THE MISREPRESENTATION OF GOD

THE MYSTERIES OF GOD EXPLAINED AND THE DISTORTION OF GOD BY RELIGION

BY SCOTT HALBERT

Introduction

The title of this book brings forth the assumption that one, there is a God, and that two He is being misrepresented. There is more to this book than simply bringing to light the massive misrepresentation of God that has existed since time began. In order to point a finger so to speak, you must also have an answer, or, a presentation of truth that battles the lies and misconceptions being promoted. My hope in writing this book is not so much to slam the misconceptions being heralded in our pulpits and in the streets, but to more importantly provide a plausible common sense refutation of these ideas in the hope that some, even if only a few, will see truth and walk away from the bondage they are in and learn to live the freedom that God has called us to in Christ.

If you are an atheist or unbeliever, and you happened to pick up this book out of curiosity because of the title; I would urge you to please read on! I believe you will read ideas and thoughts that you have never heard before, from religious people or the institutions promoting God and religion today.

As I sit here and contemplate and put to writing my thoughts and ideas of the mysteries of God and of mankind, one question comes to mind;
"Who am I to think that I have some kind of patent on truth or the way of things?"

Who would listen to me? I'm just an average guy, no degrees, no special schooling. What makes me think that I have a unique understanding of things like;
Who am I, why am I here?
If there is a God, what does he want from me?
What does he want, for me.
If there is a God why do people die and suffer?

These and Many other questions are on the minds of nearly every human being on the planet today, and have existed since the beginning of time. It is a common scenario. I don't think anyone escapes these questions and thought processes. In fact I would go so far as to say that these thoughts are a part of our DNA, built into us if you will. Questioning things is good and healthy for not only our wellbeing, but also helps us to separate lies from the truth.

So, who am I? How am I qualified to sit here and write these thoughts and present them to you as truth? I have no formal training, and the extent of my tenure as a minister/Sunday school teacher lasted only a few years before I decided that was not where I wanted to be, and that religion did not hold the answers to the questions I had been asking since I was a very young man.

So I will tell you a little bit about whom I am and let you be the judge based on that information, as well as the thoughts and ideas I will present in this short book. As to whether or not you think I have a unique understanding of truth, or that I'm just another crazy Christian who clings to the God idea because he cannot handle life without that crutch will be your decision. My purpose is not to convince you to buy into my theology. But rather, give you a perspective that few today have thought of or brought to the masses. It's not my job to convince you. I'm just a messenger. So, consider the message, and if it makes sense to you, great. If not, well, I appreciate you hearing what it is I have to say anyway.

As for who I am, I'll try to make this quick because I'm not interested in spending too much time on myself. It's the message of truth that is most important but it's also nice to know a little bit about the person whom you are allowing to enter your brain so-to speak.

As I stated before I'm just an average guy. At the time of this writing I was/am 52 years old. I grew up in a fairly large family, 3 boys and 3 girls, we liked to compare ourselves to the "Brady Bunch"! For those of you who don't know who the Brady Bunch was, they were a TV family made up of a single mom with three girls, and a single dad with three boys. They married and the show was about the transition they all went through becoming a family.

My family, similar to the Brady Bunch, is kind of a hodge podge mixture of half brothers and sisters and full brothers and sisters and it can get a little confusing. However, all of us siblings are pretty close and we don't see the half part, we are just, family. I was born in Wichita Falls Texas in 1963 on Shepard Air Force base. I was very young, maybe 1.5-2 years old when we moved to Seattle Washington. I grew up and lived there until I turned 16. My mother and father divorced when I was about 13 and all of us kids remained with her with the exception of my older brother. He was sent to live in a foster home when I was around 8 or 9 years of age. He and my mom had issues that could not be reconciled. Our family had its issues and in this regard we certainly were not like the Brady Bunch!

My mom was a very controlling woman who had issues with alcohol, and men. My dad was a hard-working man who worked for the Seattle fire department and took on side jobs in the construction industry. He also commercial fished for salmon to make ends meet for this large family. My mom didn't work outside the home, nor did she work inside the home! That's what we kids were for. Now, in all fairness I will say that she must have worked for a period of time in the home while we were babies. However once a couple of us were old enough to begin taking over the chores of the house, they were all gradually delegated to us so that my years from about age 5 to 16 I do not recall seeing my mom do much work at all. She spent most of her time on the phone with friends' chit chatting.

Don't get me wrong here, I completely agree with kids doing chores and helping their parents and learning to be productive in society. And I won't get too involved in explaining in detail my mom's methods, or the lack there-of, let's just say that we kids learned very early on to become independent because life at home sucked! In some ways however I am thankful for the way things were because all of us kids are hard- working individuals and the word entitlement does not even enter our thought processes as to how a person should conduct themselves. I will also say that with the exception of teaching my kids a good work ethic, I do not raise my children in the same manner as my parents.

At age 16 I ran away from my mother's home and lived on the streets in Yakima, Washington for a couple of weeks. I called my dad and he said I could come live with him. I couldn't live with my mom any longer. Her anger issues with men had begun to be projected on to me. At least that's how I felt.

Oh, I almost forgot! At age eleven I was attending what is still called today, Awanna, at the local Presbyterian church. Kind of a social gathering of kids where they play and learn a little about Jesus. During these classes I became a believer. The message I remember was very simple, something like, if you want to go to heaven and not hell when you die, ask Jesus into your heart and you'll go to heaven. I decided immediately I didn't want to go to hell, so it made perfect sense to ask Jesus into my heart. That was the extent of any religious training for me for quite some time.

At age 17 I joined the Air Force. I spent just under a year in the service due to a dispute over which job I had signed up for and the fact that the AF was sneakily trying to push me into a field I wasn't interested in by misrepresenting what that job entailed. I fought it and managed to eventually be discharged early with an honorable discharge.

I moved back to the state of my birth, Texas, right after being discharged and took a job at an auto parts store in the town of Tyler for about three years until I decided to go out on my own using some skills my dad had taught me in the floor covering industry when I was a kid. I have been self- employed ever since, owning many different business types from installing and selling flooring, to manufacturing concrete products, to building and owning a couple of convenience stores and a liquor store. I'm still self- employed today currently building a couple of new businesses.

My return to things religious happened at age 23. I was with the mother of my only blood child, and she had three kids from her previous marriage and she was to say the least a very difficult woman! I wanted a family so much during this time that I ignored all of the red flags that were plastered in front of me. This woman, just like my mom had men issues. Her dad was an alcoholic and she was abused, not sexually, but physically by both him and her first husband. Again, I caught the brunt of it. During my time with her I became a broken man. I turned to religion because that was what I remembered from my youth. Maybe God could help me. So I re-dedicated my life to him and began to study and learn as much as I could about him. My wife left me when I was 27 and I thank God often for her decision!

I met my second wife at age 28. She was quite a bit older than myself. She was almost the complete opposite of my first wife. More settled, more on the ball, but there were red flags there as well that turned out to be quite serious later down the road. And I of course ignored them because she was so much better than my first wife, I figured we could sort it out. After 17 years of marriage, I left her! She and I still communicate and get along because during that relationship we got custody of her granddaughter and I try to continue to be an influence in her life. I could get extremely involved in writing my bio but right now I'm simply trying to give you a basic idea of my background and experiences.

During my time with my second wife, I continued to study and research and look for a closer more informed relationship with God. I had already left the church towards the end of my first marriage. I felt as if the church was hindering my growth, and right or wrong I was bound to listen to that inner voice that was leading me to grow in my relationship with God, in the real world where I would not be influenced by someone else's version of who God was. That search continues today.

I am remarried again and to date is the best relationship I have ever experienced. It's not perfect, but it's good. I continue to seek and learn from everyday experiences, who I am and who God is and how we fit together in the whole scheme of things. You can learn some things from the past, like in the scriptures and how God dealt with mankind as recorded in those writings, but I believe we must see them for what they are, examples of how God dealt with man during those times past, but seek him in the now. We as a society have changed greatly since the times of Abraham, Moses, the disciples etc. And though God is unchanging, meaning he is the same yesterday, today and always, the way he deals with us is as diversified as the way we deal with our kids. Our kids are not all the same and they are not always the same age. We deal with our kids on the basis of their level of understanding. We deal with babies as babies, teens as teens and adults as adults. God is the same way and he knows how to reach us as we are today, whatever level we are at in our understanding. The examples set forth for us in the scriptures are certainly useful to help us understand God, but let's face it, the world and the people in it today are far different than they were five thousand years ago, or even 50 years ago!

Like I said before, I have no degrees, my education is limited. But one thing I do have is a pure desire for truth, the common sense to think for myself, the ability to be objective, and the motivation to put all of that together and go find truth.

I'm a person who believes that if you are truly interested in truth, and not what you think or want truth to be, but what truth is in its reality, and you are sincere about this, then God will not let you be led astray. In fact I will be so bold as to say that God never leads us astray! We lead ourselves astray when we buy into ideologies that mimic what we want truth to be! I will explain more in depth later in this book what I mean, but for now it's simple, I believe God wants us to know truth and the mysteries of the universe, and specifically the mystery of what the scriptures call godliness.

And when I say godliness, I do not mean our outer actions. I mean who we are in him when we believe. He wants us to be sincere in our search for truth, and be willing to swallow our pride and chunk what we think we know, when it differs from actual truth.

Come on let's face it, don't you want to know what the future holds? Not so much the future on earth, we know what that holds, we live, we work, we play and we die! But, the future beyond that. We are beings with an eternal perspective. That means that most of us, believe that in some form or fashion we will live on after death. That's why religion exists. From the beginning of time mankind has been looking for ways to please whatever higher power there is in order to be favored, helped, protected, and taken care of. If there were no God, there would be no conscience, no free will. We would be animals. Animals act on instinct, not out of free will choice. As the scriptures say, if this were true, that there was no God, we may as well eat, drink and be merry, for tomorrow we die. It means that if we are nothing but animals, then all of this doesn't matter one iota and we may as well fight and scrape for whatever we can get here on earth because when we die, it's all over and being a good person profits nothing.

Twenty seven years ago I made a decision; I closed my eyes and asked God to reveal truth to me. No matter the cost. Even if it completely tore down everything I thought truth was at that point in my life, (and believe me it did!). I was and still am sincere in that endeavor. This journey to find truth has lead me down some roads that many believers might interpret as back sliding, losing my faith etc. Nevertheless, I stopped worrying a long time ago about what people thought of me. You cannot let that mindset hinder your search for truth, because believe me it will.

 I don't believe truth is elusive. Not in the sense that it doesn't want to be revealed. But like anything in life worthwhile. It needs to be sought after. It's not going to give itself up unless you are sincere and your only agenda is to know it; to have a relationship with truth, so to speak.

Also, "There are no New Truths". Only truths that have been around forever, it just needs to be discovered, studied, tested, and once revealed, accepted.

In this book I will attempt to tackle many hard questions about life, religion, non-religion, relationships, and where we fit in this world. I will share with you my journey into truth seeking. I will be candid, and honest. I will present to you my way of explaining the truths I have discovered over the years, and, if you don't agree with my assessments, well, to hell with you! Just kidding! ☺ Lol! That's okay. Just try to have an open mind and see what happens. One thing I have learned about truth is that sometimes we're ready for it, and sometimes we're not. If you feel what I am writing to be ridiculous or out of this world, set it on the back shelf for now. We humans evolve into understanding; things we don't agree with now, can take on new meanings later in life.

So here we go! Hang on!

Chapter one

Who am I, why am I here?

Wow! Helluva a topic to start out with wouldn't you say?! Well, this question, or, topic, I believe, is the most important topic ever! Yes I said ever. Why, because inside each and every one of us this question is asked, and asked, and asked. If you say you have never contemplated this, I'll call you a liar! ☺

Folks have struggled with this topic since the beginning of time. To some degree, every person has searched for the answer to this question. Some have even ended their lives when the answer to this question seemed impossible to know or comprehend. The thought of going on when this truth seemed so unattainable, was too much for them. Stripped hope from them.

Some give up trying to understand this and create their own reality. We have many today that are so called experts on life and the hereafter and many of them have never truly searched for the answers to these topics. They believe in what sounds good to them. As a young man I bought into what I call George Burns philosophy. In his movie 'Oh God!', he preached the idea that God puts us on this earth to do with what we will. His was a, "just be good to each other", type of gospel, and everything would work out and God would be happy. And though being good to one another is certainly an admirable thing, and probably does please God, that philosophy falls way short of Gods intention for us.

Many are content not to know, because they are comfortable with their life, and do not want to disrupt it with perceived changes that understanding truth may bring about. I call this ostrich faith. Where you stick your head in the sand believing that if you don't know anything, nothing can hurt you! The Ostrich however doesn't realize that, though they have protected their head, their ass is still on the line! ☺ I don't know about you, but to me, if I'm to spend just a short time on this earth, and the rest of eternity is spent somewhere else, I'd kinda like to know about eternity and the options, wouldn't you?

The question of who we are and why we are here drives us, it motivates us, it frustrates us and makes us angry. On the flip side, to those who feel as if they understand this topic, it brings peace. No other topic, or question in the world has the power to affect our lives, good or bad, the way this one does.

So, who are we? Before I get to that, let me explain the basis of my beliefs. I am a Christian. (As if you didn't key in on that already!) ☺☐

What that means is that I buy into the explanation that this world was created by God, and that God manifested himself in the person of Jesus Christ. Now before all of you atheists and other versions of non-believers throw this book in the trash this moment, I would challenge you to keep reading. You're going to read some theories and ideas that most likely you have never heard before. Why do I say this? Because I don't hear them in organized religion! I am not religious and I do not attend church. I have my reasons for this that will most likely become apparent as you read on.

 It's also one of the reasons I told you about in the introduction that some believe me to be a 'back slider' or a 'heretic' or something along those lines. I don't concern myself with what others think, I try to follow my convictions as truth is revealed to me.

 Anyway, the way I am about to explain the question of who we are and why we are here, is not mentioned in any church I know of, with one exception in my experience; 'The Christ Life Fellowship' based in Dallas, Texas. The question of who we are and why we are here is not mentioned by televangelists, radio ministers, and aside from the writings of the folks at CLF, I've yet to read one book that explains these truths effectively.

They might preach parts of this truth, but rarely does anyone really open it up and teach truth in its entirety.

One would think that with all of the ministers and preachers and evangelists running around the world trying to save it, you would hear a proper and plausible explanation of this most desired and most important truth! But you don't. It's not preached, taught or offered. At least to the degree I am about to explain.

Why is this? Several reasons; One reason is, you can't teach what you do not know! <u>Bottom line.</u>
Am I so arrogant as to be saying that the majority of Christiandom does not understand the truths God wishes us to know? Call it what you want but that is exactly the case! Uhmm, not that I AM, arrogant and think I know everything, but most today in Christian circles do not understand truth! ☺

Truth sets people free, and free people do not need or want anyone controlling their lives with fear, guilt or any other negative motivating factor. Religion actually fears truth, at least in its entirety, because religion thinks it could not survive by teaching it fully! Religion believes that the teaching of these truths would instigate a falling away from organized religion because it believes people would run crazy wild and wouldn't support them. And they are probably right! But not for the reasons they think. Religion and religious leaders

negate the cross with this thinking. They do not trust
God for their existence, or the keeping of believers.

They do not trust Christ in the believer to keep the
believer from going hog wild into a life of sin because of
freedom in Christ. Religion doesn't understand that the
very life of God in the believer eventually moves and
motivates the believer to live an honest, moral and
decent life.
But in order for this to take place, the believer first
needs to understand that they are no longer enslaved to
the old sin nature, but are now alive, spiritually in
Christ. This process takes time to sink in. The believer
who continues to live in sin simply doesn't know who
they are. And as a result, they continue to be enslaved,
physically and mentally by the habits and practices of
the old sin nature, even though they are spiritually alive
in Christ!

 We humans tend to be insecure. We are always
looking for accolades. We care too much about what
others think of us. We want to be the celebrity, we
want to be liked, loved and thought of as smart or
beautiful or whatever. We are all guilty of that,
including myself. Remember what I said about truth, it
won't allow you to find it or understand it until your
motives are pure.
 I remember my religious days. I was training to be a
minister, preaching occasionally, teaching Sunday
school and home studies, things that all good Christians

do right? Well, I remember sitting at my desk one day studying. The following Sunday I was to give the message because the main pastor was out of town. There was another minister in training at the church I attended and he and I rotated giving the message when he wasn't there, thus giving us experience at public speaking. While I was sitting there wondering what topic I would speak on, I caught my self-thinking,

"*I wonder if I will preach as good as Shaw does*!" Shaw was the name of the other minister in training.

When it dawned on me what I was thinking, I got a little angry with myself. I couldn't believe this had become a competition in my mind of who was the better preacher! I sat there, disgusted with myself. I apologized to God and asked him to reveal truth to me. To help rid me of this insecurity, and need to be liked and accepted. I told him I didn't care what the cost was. I just wanted to know him, to know truth. My heart was set right that day in regards to my search for truth. 😇 I gave up the idea of preaching and the ministry as a vocation. I decided that was not the road for me. I realized that I did not know God. Not really. Oh I was saved, I was a believer. But in the same way babies do not know their parents, I did not really know God, and I wanted to. I wanted the truth. Somehow for me, I knew that journey did not involve organized religion, at least for me. So I left the church and began my journey to know truth, to know God, outside of it. 🕊️⛪️

Am I saying that everyone should up and leave their church? Not at all. But if you feel your church is holding you back, keeping you from growing and understanding truth, then maybe that is what is best. I have found that churches may be good at getting people to believe initially, but much like our government today, they keep you from growing.

They believe they cannot support their buildings and ministries if the congregation is taught they are free to live life as they see fit. Just like our government wishes to control every aspect of our lives, and believes they know better, what is good for us than we do. The church is similar. They don't believe God can keep them, and motivate them purely out of love, to live life properly.

Another reason you don't hear truth today is inexperience. So many times young people are thrust into the ministry to teach things they do not know, or understand. Don't get me wrong, these people can learn as they go, but like I said before, you cannot teach what you do not know. So they wind up preaching and teaching from a curriculum and give messages and lessons that are pre-set for them by someone else's thoughts, ideas and convictions.

So you ask the question, why are we still not hearing truth from those who have been in the ministry for many years? Good question! We've already talked about pure motivation and sincerity being needed for truth to reveal itself, and in many cases that is the problem. However, a few are looking for an easy life away from hard work. Still others look to go big time and profit financially from religion. 🏔️ ☐ 💰 Manipulating people with fear, greed, or guilt is big business these days!   Then there are some, who actually want to make a difference but are deterred by fear of bucking the system. ☺ It's easier to just go with the flow and teach what has been taught for years in the format it has been taught for years.

 Searching for truth is an adventure. 🚴. It takes effort to investigate the mystery. Yes, truth is a mystery. Webster's defines mystery as;

 "A religious truth that one can know only by revelation and cannot fully understand".

 What does it mean to know by revelation? Revelation is the means of revealing a truth or truths to someone. Have you ever had something just click for you? For the longest time you could not understand it, but then all of the sudden you get it! That's revelation. You cannot understand spiritual truth unless the Holy Spirit reveals it. That means I can explain, teach and preach to you all day long, but if you're not ready to understand it, and the Spirit doesn't reveal it, you won't! Sometimes, you get it, you know it, but you cannot explain it.

So why bother you ask? Simple, no one knows when you're ready or not ready to receive, or to have a truth revealed to you. Only the Spirit knows this. So it makes perfect sense to continue to teach, preach etc. because you never know, you just might be ready. This fact also takes the load off of me, or anyone teaching truth; I'm just a messenger, the rest is between yourself and God.

My sister and I talked back and forth for five years about the same truths that had been revealed to me, and she just didn't understand. She struggled with what religion had been telling her through the mechanisms of fear, guilt and greed. These can be a real hindrance to growth as I explained earlier. Then one day she called me and said brother, I finally get it! And from that point on she easily understood everything I had been trying to help her see for those five years! It finally clicked for her. She was at last ready. And once things began to click, everything began to fall into place for her. It was like a flood, a peaceful flood. When she stopped caring what the other folks at church would say about her journey for truth, and like myself, no longer cared about the potential cost of knowing and living truth, truth began to be revealed to her. ✳

Many evangelists and preachers get comfortable and cling to norms. I've walked out on many messages because I kept hearing the same old crap; mostly topics dealing with a believer's outer actions and useless tricks to curb sin in our lives. Or, exhortations to go and claim the world for Christ, even though that endeavor never has been on Gods agenda!

I've debated with ministers over topics to no avail. Do this and God will bless you, God didn't bless you because you didn't do this! Or you didn't do it the right way! Follow these steps to a fulfilled life. Pray these words and God will listen, and so on and so on, makes me sick! 😵. This is what I call Formula Christianity. It isn't any wonder non-believers think we're crazy idiots and want nothing to do with us! And we, simply pass it off as those idiot non-believers, how could they not respond to our message, when in reality it is our message that is pushing them away! 😕 I believe that if truth were presented, simply, honestly and correctly, people would be beating the doors down to get a taste. ➤

I once had a conversation with a new pastor at a church. He listened, and actually agreed with me on everything I pointed out regarding truth! We were discussing the topic of being saved by grace and not by adherence to the law. Like I said he agreed with my assessments of that topic. But he went on to explain to me why he didn't fully teach it. He said, "Scott, you're right, the believer has freedom in Christ. But you have to add a little law to keep them in line!" He actually said that! ☹ Even though he claimed to know truth, He didn't believe it! He did not trust Christ in the believer! So his answer was to have a new person in Christ, who was designed to live in freedom from laws that could not save them, continue to live by those laws and not by the life of God that was now in that believer! That's like having an insurance policy on your salvation from an insurance company that has gone broke, but kept selling policies with no intention or ability to honor the policy! 🙁 The law being that insurance policy.

 We have failed in our delivery of the truth because we do not seek the truth and because we do not believe the truth. And for these reasons, we do not know the truth. We have packaged up a gospel, 🎁 that quite frankly has people thinking they would rather choose hell than buy into that ridiculous religion if those are the choices! We have commercialized it and made truth unappealing and ridiculous. We have sensationalized it, capitalized on it, and in so doing we have misrepresented God in the worst possible ways. And people shun churches and religion because of this.

 Many years ago I was working out if town and was teamed up on a construction job with a biker. Jesse was his name. Jesse was a pretty rugged dude, (hell I'm a pretty rugged dude myself!) or so people say. I could tell after a few conversations that there was more to him than his rugged exterior. After a few days of work and getting comfortable with one another our conversations somehow turned to religion. Jesse told me that he did not attend church because something was missing there. He had tried many of them, different denominations and just couldn't bring himself

to go anymore. He said he felt a little bad about this, like maybe he was disappointing God. Underneath Jessie's rough exterior was a decent man and he claimed to love God but he just couldn't do the church thing. Freedom was missing there he said, but he struggled with being taught that, unless you went to a church, you were back sliding and could lose your salvation, or at the least God would be very unhappy with you. I proceeded to explain to Jesse, just as I am about to explain to you, who we are and why we are here, in a way he had never heard before in religion. And as I explained to him how I believed things were, and gave him some examples and drew a couple of rough drawings that might help him understand, I saw tears in his eyes! ☺. Not sad tears, but of relief. That caught me by surprise. I was not expecting that kind of reaction from this tough guy.
I asked him if he was okay and he replied,

 "I've never heard anyone explain the gospel the way you have just done."

 He went on to say that he understood now why he had felt the way he had for so many years and, why truth had been so elusive. 🐎. Jesse found some truth, and at least for that day, it set him free. 🗽 The reason I say, "at least for that day" is because truth is a daily experience, and can be forgotten. And even though you can never cease to become a child of God once you believe, "God does not abort his kids" you can however loose the peace in your life that comes from understanding what it means to be free in Christ, if you forget or allow untruths to enter your thinking and take hold.

 Years ago after I left the church I was attending and learning to be a minister at, a friend of mine who still taught Sunday school to teens there called me, and asked if I would substitute for him the following Sunday. I agreed under one condition, that I could teach what I wanted to teach and not from the program. He agreed. So I showed up that Sunday, gave a basic explanation to the class explaining to them what I am explaining to you in this book.

One of the students that was there was a trouble maker. He was the cool kid who didn't need anyone, and I believe he was there only because his parents made him attend. Tough kid, you know the type. Hard to handle, always getting in trouble, usually angry about something. Class ended and he was the last one to walk out and he stopped at my desk. I asked him what was up, and he proceeded to thank me for the lesson. Said he had never heard anyone explain in such a simple way what he had been trying to figure out himself. I'd love to tell you he lived happily ever after, but I never saw him again. They never asked me back at that church! I don't know how his life turned out but I do know something clicked for him that day. My hope is that he continued his search.

When you are sincere, you may not understand or know how to articulate what you're looking for, but you know it when you hear it! Your soul, your mind can differentiate between truth and lies when you are sincere in your search for truth. And when you don't get truth, life can be very frustrating. It's like a craving that will only be satisfied by what you are craving! Many people today cannot explain why they feel empty, angry, frustrated, even when attending church. It's almost like we have this detector in us, not unlike a metal detector, and it only goes off when the right material is presented to it.   And the longer we go without that detector going off, the more frustrating life becomes. 😖

So, now having given you a glimpse of where I am coming from, here we go,
 Who am I, and why am I here?

 In order for you to be able to understand what I am about to say, a couple of things need to be in place. First, you need to have a belief that there is something, someone, higher than our selves. To me that is God. You need to believe in the concept of love, and that all positive things flow and are motivated by love. If you can at least agree on these things you have a chance of understanding what I am writing about. If not, that's okay, I urge you to read ahead anyway, you never know, things just might click. 🙂

The questions who am I and why am I here, really should be reversed! You can't really know who you are without first knowing why you are here. My opinion. But I think it's valid. So having said that;

"Why am I here?"

Quite simply, you are here because of love. Really, you ask? Yep, that's it! In a nutshell that's it! Don't worry I will explain further. You see there is a person, who so desired to love and to be loved that he decided to risk everything in hopes of bringing about the one thing he desired more than anything. Love. And that person is God, (I know you had that figured out already but I had to say it!). ☺

God, being the creator, formed in his mind a plan before the earth was ever created. Before you and I were ever created. He had already created many spiritual beings. Angels, etc. and though these beings he created were beautiful, and they sang to him and they worshipped him, and followed his every instruction perfectly, it simply was not enough. Something was missing. Much like my friend Jesse talked about when he would attend churches and still would feel empty. ☹

You see the Angels did these things for God because they were created to do so. There was never a choice for them, that is who they are; programmed, if you will.

Yet even in their beauty and perfection God did not find what he was looking for. He wasn't satisfied. So he created another angel, a special angel. He gave him the name Lucifer. It is written he was the most beautiful and most powerful angel ever created. But God gave him something else. Something no angel previous to him had ever received. God gave Lucifer free will. He gave him a soul.

I can just imagine what was going on in Gods mind when he decided to do this! He must have thought something like, "I am about to give one of my creations the ability to either love me, or hate me. I am giving this creation of mine the ability to choose right or wrong, to do either good or evil." And it must have been a bit stressful for God. For the first time, ever, another entity had the power to choose!

Wow! Can you imagine? Everything before was controlled; everything in its place, never had there been a lie, a murder, theft, adultery, any sin. And now, it all changed.

In some ways it is similar to raising a child. When they are young we have relative control over them, but that day comes when they are no longer under our control and are completely responsible for themselves. It's a scary day for most parents. I know the analogy breaks down because even little children have free will. But it is just about as close as I can come to helping you see what God may have been feeling at the time.

So, what do you think happened? You guessed it!
Lucifer became prideful, arrogant, un-controllable and
decided He didn't need God... And he wanted Gods
stuff! Sound like anyone to you? Maybe that teenager
you tried to raise properly?
 Anyway, as the story goes God kicked him out, and sent
some buddies with him.

 Now God is back to square one! He still does not have
what he wants most, love. He now knows that a mere
creation, even as beautiful and perfect as Lucifer was,
even with the power of free will, cannot give him what
he wants. There is but one option left, along with being
created with a body, and a soul, and with free will!
Somehow God needs to be able to put in that being a
part of himself. Why not just do it you ask? There are a
couple of reasons actually as to why that would not
work.

 First, it would be no different than when he created the
Angels. They did what they did because they were
created to do those things. You cannot achieve true
love from a programmed being. (I know some men and
women who would beg to differ from me!) but
truthfully you can't.

Second, forcing yourself on someone else either
physically, mentally, or spiritually, is rape, and that is
not who God is. There is risk in love. To achieve true

love both parties must choose each other. They must open themselves to one another, and accept one another as they are. So, God began to formulate a plan; a plan that would allow the creation the option of either accepting his love, or rejecting it. Along with that plan was a means by which God could and would place his own life and nature in the creation. One problem, his prototype if you will, Lucifer, had shown him that the odds were, the creation, apart from already having Gods life and nature in it, would most likely choose wrong. Quite a pickle he was in to say the least.

Can you imagine being in this position? On the one hand, the creation needs a part of God in them in order to enter into a loving relationship with him, but on the other hand, for the creation to get Gods life and nature in them requires a choice, a decision to allow that to take place. And the creation choosing that, is at best 50/50. Probably worse odds than that.

One writer tells us that God chose us to be "In Christ" before the foundation of the world. Being in Christ means to have the very life and nature of God in us. His choosing us to be in Christ means that Christ was to be the vehicle that brought creation and creator together. Remember, Christ is the very life and nature of God. God chose the method and the means, there is no other way. This is his way.

I know people who actually get angry about this! How can God be so arrogant that we have to do things HIS way? It's not arrogance folks! It's simplicity. By having only one way, we are less likely to get confused over the matter. How many of you would instruct your child that the way to get home from school, or the store, or anywhere for that matter, would tell them, "don't worry, all roads lead home!" It doesn't matter which way you go, you'll get here. Of course you wouldn't do that, would you? Neither does God. His way is simple, singular, and direct. **In Christ**.

He figured out that us being in Christ was the only way to achieve his goal. So what that means is what I have been telling you, that creation needs a part of God in it in order to enter into the loving relationship he desired. The dilemma is getting that part of him in us without forcing us or programming it into us. This must be a courtship, a courtship based on love, and a courtship willing to let go in the event the creation chose to reject his offer.

I have to interject here, religion has done such a poor job throughout the centuries forwarding this truth to the masses. It has come across as a message of fear, and judgment, or greed. Trust God and he'll give you miracles and riches! Or reject God and go to hell! Let me ask all of you married men out there, when you courted your wife did you tell her that if she didn't marry you, you would beat her, humiliate her, or kill her? Or did you try to buy her love? Of course you didn't! How far do you think that would get you? Not far I suspect and if you did try those methods, how did that work out for you? And if it did get her to accept you using those methods, it was most certainly not based on mutual love for one another. I would be willing to bet that you wooed her, you said loving things to her, you gave her an occasional gift because you loved her, and you treated her with love and respect. That is how you win true love. Not with threats, and not with the promise of riches and miracles trying to buy her love.

 But on the flip side, if she decided not to accept your love, and she has every right to do that, then she has no right to share in your life, your love, or your blessings, does she?
 You see, God does not condemn anyone. If the creation chooses not to enter into the relationship that he has offered in love and sincerity, the creation condemns itself from ever sharing in the benefits of those things. This folks, is the definition of Hell! Separation from God is Hell. Why, because only in Christ is there peace, joy, and true love. And without him, those things do not exist. God will not force you. He will not make you do anything you don't want. But I ask, why wouldn't you want to?
 Now if it was presented to you based on fear or guilt I can understand why you wouldn't want to. But the message wasn't supposed to be that way.
 So back to my explanation... God needed to figure out a way to get a part of himself in the creation so that his love for us, could be reciprocated.

It was a sticky situation. And there is more to this. You see, even after the creation believed, accepted and trusted Gods invitation, one more obstacle was in the way. "Sin"

God, being perfect, cannot fellowship with sin. And we are born in sin. I know, I'm gonna have to explain that one to you.

I think most people are familiar with the account of the creation of Adam and Eve, the first human beings. Nevertheless I'll recap for those who haven't.

After creating the earth and everything in it, God created Adam and Eve and placed them in a garden in which to live. During this time he actually spent time with them. He was able to do this because as of yet there was no sin in them. They walked together, had conversations etc. God made fruit bearing trees for them to eat and streams for water etc. He told them they could eat from any tree in the garden they wished with one exception, the tree of the knowledge of good and evil. He forbade them from eating from this tree telling them if they did, they would die. Time went on, who knows how long but one day eve was near the tree and was beckoned by a serpent. A very beautiful serpent that was also a smooth talker so the story goes, and the serpent asked her why they never ate from that tree. Eve responded, telling him God forbade it and warned them that if they did, they would die. The serpent laughed a little and told eve that God had lied to them. He told her that eating from that tree would actually make her and Adam just like God, knowing all things. Basically he told her God was holding out on them.

Eve believed the serpent and ate some of the fruit from that tree. She then took some to Adam, repeated what the serpent said and he ate as well.

(women are always talking us into things we shouldn't do!) 😃

Anyway, they both immediately felt guilty and ashamed; for the first time they recognized their nakedness and made clothing from leaves.

Later, God showed up for his walk with them and saw that they were partially hidden in the bushes. He asked them why they hid, they said because they were naked. He asked them who told them they were naked, and they divulged that they had eaten from the tree he forbade them to and that was when they realized their nakedness.

They disobeyed God, and did not believe him. They sinned. Sin is the absence, or, lack of perfection in ones actions and thoughts. God, being perfect, could no longer walk with them.

There is so much more in this story and we will get to that later. At this time I wanted to show you what brought about mankind's separation from God. By the way, when God said they would die, he didn't mean a physical death. You see separation from God is a death, it is spiritual death. The end result of Adam and Eve’s sin was that all of mankind from that point on was and is born in spiritual death; Separated from God, by sin.

This means that our spirit part is now filled with the nature of the one whom Adam and Eve believed. That serpent in the garden was Lucifer.
His Spirit died when he was cast out by God for rejecting him and attempting to usurp Gods throne. He is known as the Father of sin and death. You could say that Lucifer is the spiritual father of all mankind until a person hears the gospel and believes. The moment a person believes, their old sin nature, or, the nature of Lucifer in them, is replaced by Gods nature. His life, which we now refer to as, Christ in us.

So how does God give us the ability to listen, and believe, and accept his love without a part of him in us; while we are still spiritually dead? That vehicle is Faith. Another writer tells us that God gives to each man a measure of faith; just enough to be able to believe and to accept his gift of love and life. There is more however! In order for us to be able to exercise that bit of faith, the justification for this because of sin, needed to be dealt with and here is how he did that.

First off when you are the creator of the universe, and everything in it, you get to make the rules. I've tried my best to teach this to all of the children I have had the privilege of having a part in raising. It tickles me when my step son William doesn't want to eat what we want to when we go out, or at home and he either wants something different or wants to go somewhere else! First thing I ask him is does he have the money to pay for the meal! He of course answers no! He's only eight you see and he makes that fact abundantly clear to us! He goes on to say that it is not fair that we don't let him choose the meals. I explain to him that it's perfectly fair because we pay for the meals, and if he wants to choose our meals he needs to be able to pay for them! Some of you parents may think this is harsh. I don't think so. Our job as parents is to prepare our children for a harsh world that does not care about them. We do our children a disservice by catering to them and coddling them. When we do those things, they enter that harsh world totally unprepared for the way things are.

So, God makes the rules. One of his rules is that sin must be paid for. The consequence of sin, is death. And the currency that justifies God being able to forgive it, is a life sacrifice. Pretty expensive if you ask me! 🙂 So expensive In fact, that not a person in the whole world past or present has the ability to pay that bill. Not collectively, not individually. So how did it get paid?

Let me ask you something, have you ever seen a down & outer that could not pay for their own meal? And you bought them a meal? It's kind of like that only multiplied a thousand times over. God sticks to his own rules. He has to because he is just.

So he didn't just waive it because he was God. But because he is honorable, and because he knew we could not afford, nor did we have the credit to pay that debt, He agreed to pay the price for our sin in order to open the door again to fellowship with us, so we could become a part of his family. God allowed his only son, the second person in the trinity, Christ, to offer himself as that sacrifice for the payment of our sins! Yes, God had a son. His son was his life, his nature and according to certain writings, he had been with God from the beginning.

How can this be? You ask. Well, God, being God, can do things that we do not comprehend with our finite minds. According to different writers there is only one God. However, the one God acts in three specific capacities. They are listed as, God the father, God the Son, and God the Holy Spirit. Many call this group the trinity. (Fits anyway!)

It can be confusing, but you can understand this truth at some point. He gave us glimpses of this phenomenon. One such glimpse is how we were created. It is said that we are created in Gods image. I believe that to mean that we as well as God, are tri-partate, meaning, we also have three parts to our creation. They are as follows;

Body
Soul
Spirit

(See illustration 1)

The spirit and the soul are often confused with each other. I'll break the three parts down for you real quick. The body is pretty much self- explanatory. It is our physical bodies that we see and feel.

The soul is our mind, our will, and our emotions. It's our personality, the way we think, the way we are motivated, and the way we react to different stimulus like love, fear, anger, peace, joy etc.

The spirit is the part of Adam and Eve that died, or more properly explained, was completed in spiritual death, when they believed the serpent instead of God. They were still alive in body and soul. And because we take on all characteristics and attributes of our parents, mankind has been born in this state of spiritual death since Adam and Eve. It's also called the sin nature as I stated earlier. No one is born innocent! Don't believe me? If you currently have little children or if you have children that have grown up, I would like to ask you a question. Did you have to teach them to lie, to steal, to hurt others, to be selfish? I already know the answer, it's no! Those things come naturally to every human being born into this world. What you do have to teach them is the opposite of those attributes, like, honesty, selflessness, kindness, responsibility, and so on. Our very existence screams the truth of what I am telling you.

So, back to Gods dilemma; how to pay for our sins that required a death payment? Making us pay would have been counterproductive to his plan. Besides, you must be alive spiritually in order to be able to pay a debt that is spiritual in nature. The only spiritually living beings at this time were the trinity! So it had to be one of them that paid the bill.

 I know some of you are confused right now thinking I am saying there are three Gods. I'm not saying that. There is only one God, he simply manifests, or, represents himself in three capacities. We can actually do that as well! How? I can represent myself as a father because I have children. I can also represent myself as a son, because I have parents, and I can also represent myself as a husband, because I have a wife. One of the reasons the Jews allowed Jesus to be crucified is because Jesus claimed to be the son of God. And in doing so they knew he was actually claiming to be God, come in the flesh. So it is The Son, Christ, who stepped forward and gave his life as payment for our sins. It must have broken Gods heart to allow this, but he did.

 There's more! Not only did Christ spiritually die for our sins, he died physically and in his soul as well. God needed to understand our plight, and the only way for that to happen, is to experience our plight. So Christ became a man, and lived as we do, and suffered as we do, and died as we do. I need to clarify something here. When I say he died we understand that he died physically, as well as his soul, but how could he die spiritually? Being the Son of God and spiritually alive with the very nature and life of God? One writer tells us that when he died, his spirit and soul went to hell for a short time. He was separated from God his father during this time. And since being separated from God defines Hell, it also defines spiritual death, which Christ experienced, even though briefly. But being the son of God, Hell, or spiritual death could not hold him.

 Again, this means that the soul and spirit cannot experience peace, joy, love and all of the blessings God extends to us if we do not choose to accept his love. By choosing not to accept his love, we condemn ourselves to separation from him. It's our choice. However, by the same token, if we choose to accept his love, his life, we will be a part of his family for eternity. And with that comes the privilege of having his peace, his love and all the blessings that come with being a member of that family. It also makes us privy to the family secrets! ☺ You heard me! By becoming a child of God through belief in him, we get to see and understand truths that are invisible to us otherwise. The third person of the trinity comes into play here. Once we believe and our sin nature is swapped for a new nature, Gods nature, life spiritually if you will, the Holy Spirit becomes our teacher. He is the revealer. I don't often quote verses from the bible but in this instance I will. In the book of John, chapters 14-16, Jesus taught this truth. He told us that when he was gone, the spirit of truth would then be available as teacher to those who believed.

 What does this mean? It means that until you believe, and your sin nature is removed and replaced by Gods Nature, Christ in us, you cannot understand truth, or anything involving the workings of God! The Hell you say! Yep, that's what I say. Come on now it makes perfect sense. Would you allow a stranger into your home, to learn the family business and its secrets if they were not family? Of course you wouldn't. And neither does God.

It is for this reason that I can boldly proclaim that people like say Steven Hawking, who is an admitted atheist, as great as his mind is, cannot and does not understand the mysteries of God, his plan, or why you and I are even here! I'll probably get some fan mail for that statement! But it's true people! Mr. Hawking may be able to understand the mechanics of the universe, to a certain degree, but he completely missed the author of the universe. And that he's a person

who loves him and wishes he would take that leap of faith, and believe and become a part of the biggest family ever. Can you imagine the things Mr. Hawking could know?! If he exercised that tiny bit of faith God gave him.

Anyway, back to the payment for sin. It was Jesus's death that set things right and satisfied Gods just nature. He was the currency for our sin debt. Paid, once, and for all. So you ask, if he paid for all, why are not all saved? Why is believing a necessary action if he paid everyone's debt? Come on, you already know the answer! But I'll repeat it anyway. Even though my debt is paid, I profit nothing from it if I first off, know nothing about it, second, if I reject the benefits of my debt being paid. We can refuse to have our debt paid.

I have to say this. I personally do not understand atheists! I have much more to tell you but so far I have shown you a loving God. Who needs us as much as we need him! Wait a sec, God needs us? Well, he doesn't need us for him to be God, but he does need us in order to be a Father of many children, and, to experience being loved as he loves us. What I don't understand about the atheist is that their message is a message of ZERO, hope! It's just you. There is nothing after you die. We are just electrical charges that cease to exist, or, go off into the universe and are absorbed by it, when the body dies, according to one atheist I spoke to. I would be so depressed all the time if that were true. I simply do not understand going through life, having no hope for eternity. Most atheists are actually very strong and intelligent mentally. You have to be in order to live your life with any sense of happiness and peace, with that belief system.

And then there are those who believe in God, but hate him! Don't want anything to do with him. I blame a lot of that on religion. Certainly the individual holds some responsibility for their own belief, but religion has so misrepresented God, that in some ways I don't completely blame the folks that feel this way. No one has explained to them the "why" of things. And so because of this, religion has painted a harsh and cruel

God who condemns people to hell just because they won't do what he wants. People actually believe that God kills their loved ones! I hear it all the time, "Why did God take my Mom, or Dad, or some other loved one". And they hate him for it! I'm going to deal with this topic directly in another chapter. Right now I'm just bringing up the example.

So let's re-cap. God, the creator of the universe, desires to have a relationship based on mutual love and respect. He has beings that already worship him, and do whatever he asks of them and that is not enough. He creates another being similar to the Angels and gives that being free will. That being disappoints him and stomps all over his love and grace and rejects God. God learns from this experience that creation, even with free will won't choose his gift of life and love. So he creates another being who has a capacity for the kind of love he seeks, (that's us) only he knows that his new creation will also reject him. He gives us enough faith to listen to his message of love and grace, yet still leaves in place free will, so that we're able to make our own choice, making possible a relationship between God and man. God also allows his Son to settle the sin debt mankind had with him so that all of this could be possible.

Like I said earlier, I see a God who needs us as much as we need him and is willing to cover all of the cost of this relationship. He doesn't need us to be the God he is, but he does need us for him to be a Father, and to have the reciprocal love he desires so much.

Folks this is a love story if I have ever seen one. How could anyone, learning of his love for us, want to reject it? Unless, you believe that all of this is just a fairytale made up by folks who want to control you! I can see how one might think this. Especially the way religion has portrayed God. Religion has made God out to be an egotistical power monger who only cares about his wants and needs, and what he can get out of you. I get folks questioning a God like that. I would too.

But what about a God who requires nothing from you, except trust! Simply that you believe? What about a God who so loved us that he provided everything in order to reconcile us to him? How many of you who wanted a family, a wife and children, felt that deep need to be loved by someone and to love them in return? Most of us have felt that. That my friend is exactly, how God feels. Remember, we are created in his likeness. Why wouldn't we share the same feelings and emotions that he has? And the desires he has.
I see a God who provided everything, paid for everything, sacrificed everything in order for us to become members of his amazing family. What about a God like that? Wouldn't you want to know a God like that?

So that's the "Why are we here".

Now to the "**Who we are**".

 Earlier in this chapter I touched on this with the information regarding our creation. Now I will go into more depth. We are created in Gods image in the sense that we have three parts to us, body, soul and spirit. That's the mechanics of it, but what does all that mean? Well for starters, it means that we were specifically created for a purpose. First off lets back up a bit and look at our creation again. The account of creation says that God took earth, formed it and breathed life into it. Then he named the creation Adam; which means "Man". He gave Adam dominion over all of the earth and its inhabitants; the animals, fish and birds. Let me interject something here because it ties in with who we are and our being created in the image and likeness of God.

 We are builders aren't we? We love to create buildings, parks, habitats, I love aquariums and I have actually built many of them. Where do you think we get these tendencies? We are just like God in this respect, and many others. I can see God getting all excited about what he was creating, the landscape, the oceans, the animals, us! Like a big terrarium! Animals don't do these things, nor fish or birds. Sure, some of them can build little structures in which to live, but none of them have the creativity to do even a minuscule amount if what we are able to do. It is Gods creativity that is inherently in mankind. He is the original builder, architect and creator. And he gave us these abilities as well.

 So back to Adam, after placing all of the earth and its critters in Adams care, God realized that Adam, being created in Gods image, would want to share this with someone. So the writer says that God put Adam to sleep and performed the first recorded operation!   Bet you weren't expecting that were ya? Anyway, while Adam was asleep God opened his flesh, took one of his ribs, and from that rib he created a woman; a help mate for Adam, the opposite of Adam, female and named her Eve.

 Now, one would think that God would have been done with creation at this point. But remember, God is still working on a family. And at this point Adam and Eve are just creations. But remember, the major thing about their design that was different from all other creatures, is that God created them with spiritual capacity. You see Adam and Eve had bodies, they had a soul, which is their personalities, which animals have as well, even though the soul of an animal is different than ours. The soul remember, is our mind, will and emotions. Adam and Eve had the ability to be spiritual beings as well as being fleshly beings.
Something no other creation could claim. However their spirit part had not yet been finished. Though they were perfect, they just weren't done yet!

Our spirit part, or the part of us that can contain spiritual life, is the part of Adam and Eve that God left empty because he couldn't fill it! Not without permission from them. God set his own parameters regarding this transaction because it was key to the birth of true love in mankind for him.

So, who are we?

We are created beings with a spiritual ability, or, capacity might be a better term. Unlike any other critter, and unlike any other spiritual being ever created. Including Angels and the like. We were made to be loved, and to be able to love our creator on a level that no other being can claim! That level is not just the status of a servant, or a good friend, or even an adoption. That level is one of family, birthed spiritually into the family of God. Religion would have us believe that God wants our obedience, and servitude. Not so, he wants our love. Given the alternative, and that being separation from God where peace, love and trust is absent, why would a person not wish to at least research and consider this option for their eternity?

And why are we here?

We are here because our Heavenly Father wants kids. He wants family. When we look at our kids we see ourselves. That's what God wants. He wants to see himself in us, as us. That is what fulfills God! The same thing fulfills us. It's one of the reasons we have children. We want to see ourselves in our children.

So, We, in Christ, fulfill the creator of the universe and all things in it! And he fulfills us. This my friend is the secret, the mystery of the universe!
 When you apply this knowledge, everything begins to come in to focus. Things begin to make sense.

 It's taken me 35 years of searching to come to this point of understanding, and I know there is more to come. Join with me in this journey, I challenge you! ☺

Chapter 2

The misrepresentation of God

I mentioned earlier in chapter one that religion has misrepresented God for centuries, and in this chapter I would like elaborate on that topic.

I read about a celebrity the other day who at one point in their life become a Christian. They went on to say that over the course of four years in church all they experienced was judgement, and as well some improper behavior from some of the congregation. This particular person gave up on being a Christian and is now claiming to be an atheist because of these experiences.

Too often we hear of things like this happening. And unfortunately God is usually the one who gets the bad rap.

I've been self-employed all of my life and I have had to rely on others to represent me and my companies. Over the years I have had many that have worked for me that have very poorly represented who I am and what I am about. I've had to pay for many mistakes and promises made by those who represented me, even though I myself either never condoned the behavior, or the subpar workmanship. Nevertheless, I have had to pay thousands of dollars over the years to fix, repair or refund to customers who were not happy with what my representatives did or said or failed to do or say.

Now don't get me wrong, I realize this comes with the territory. Nobody can represent you like you; and when you have to rely on others to do that, you always leave yourself vulnerable to being misread, misquoted, and therefore completely misunderstood. It sucks. But it's part of the deal. When I find out someone is misrepresenting me in such ways, I fire them. Simple, right? However the damage is done and still needs to be addressed. So I pick up the pieces and try to salvage my reputation.

Well, it's different with God. He can't just fire somebody. Well, he could, he's God right? But he doesn't. He not only made new life available to decent people, people who are sincerely searching for him, but also to those who act less than honorable, well, let's just say it, downright shitty! He came for all, he loves us all, his life is available to all. Not just to good people, but to the liars, the thieves, the murderers, the rapist, the pedophiles, and yes, even to the Democrats. ☹ Just kidding there! But seriously, to the democrats as well. ☹

And guess what we do? We misrepresent him. Some of it is out of ignorance, some out of inexperience; some is downright nasty and malicious. But we misrepresent him. Religion misrepresents him the worst, in my opinion.

Still to this day I get people, even friends who get angry when God is mentioned! Because their experience of him from religion was not what it was supposed to be. Bringing up The subject of God can in some instances ruin a relationship. It all depends on the experience of the person you are talking to, and whether their experience was good or bad.

I hear this all the time;

"If there is a God why does he let bad things happen?" *"If there is a God why did he take my loved one too early?"* *"If there is a God why are there wars and people who rise up and commit genocide and other horrible acts towards other humans?"* *"If there is a God, why does he allow some people who claim to be ministers do the despicable things they do?"* And on and on.

Some People believe that God, if he exists, is nothing more than an egotistical maniac who enjoys lording his god-ship over the puny creation! Kind of like in Greek mythology; In Greek mythology the gods are actually portrayed as being just that; Nothing more than super beings with almost psychotic tendencies. If this were true about God, why would He have given us free will? Why would he invite us puny humans into a relationship with him, to share in his life and nature for all eternity?

If God were like the gods in Greek mythology, or as hateful as many believe after dealing with religion, what would be the point in offering us eternal life and place in his family?

Many people believe that because there is evil in this world, and bad things happen to good people, that God is indifferent and sadistic and doesn't care about anyone but his own ego. It is thought that because there are those who, in the name of religion do terrible things, that God must not only not care, but is actually ok with the horrible things people do to each other as long as it is done to unbelievers. This couldn't be farther from the truth. I do however understand this perception. Because most religious leaders past and present simply do not understand what they are attempting to teach! They don't know God. They may know some things about God, that he created the world, that he sent his son to experience the plight of man and to be the payment for our sin. But they don't know God intimately. They don't understand that God is like us in many ways because he created us to be like him in many ways. That he needs us, as much as we need him. That he does not condemn us but rather provided the way for us to be reconciled to him in Christ, but only if we choose that path, only if we want that position.

I got off track a bit there, so back to this perception so many have today that God is a sadistic prick who cares about nothing but himself because he allows evil to run rampant in the world. There is an answer to this misperception. And the answer is going to blow your mind! ☹

"These issues, are not Gods fault! They are ours! We are at fault! Why? Here it goes!

 "Because we had a hand in our own creation! Yes, it's true, we helped God finish our creation.

 The hell you say!?   Really, it's true. We helped God create us! But we screwed our part up!

Here is the explanation.

 Do you remember when I told you God created us in his image and likeness? And do you remember I explained to you that part of what that means, is that we are tri-partate just like him? Having a body, a soul and a spirit? Okay so you remember. But do you also remember that I said there was one part of us that was not completed? The spirit part of man? Is it coming to you yet? The only parts of our creation that God completed were our bodies, and our souls. He only gave us spiritual capacity, not spirituality, he did not complete that part of us. Kinda like buying a new car. Nowadays you can get options on cars and if you don't want some of those options you don't have to get em.

Now, that car still has the capability of having that option. And should you choose at some later date you can get that option, because your car is made to receive it.

Are you seeing where I'm heading now? So, God made us perfect, remember, but he made us incomplete. He set it up so that only by our free will choice, would we receive the option, if you will.

So our part in our own creation is our God given ability to choose life or death. To choose what our spiritual capacity would be filled with. Adam and Eve made the first choice that affected all of mankind. They finished Gods creation of mankind, but they did so in a negative way. Negative is a mild word, let's just say it, they f#%!d up! 😁. Can I say that? 😬

However, in Gods great mercy he provided that we all, each individually would not have to suffer the negative effects of the choice of Adam and Eve forever. We have a second choice. Or, second chance. The power of that second choice will either bring us into life, or keep us in the spiritual death we are in from birth, because of our ancestors Adam and Eve. This is the reason that we have all sorts of evil going on this world. This is the reason a person can choose to either commit an act of evil, or not. And the reason God does not, cannot take that choice away from that individual, there must be the contrast of good or evil in order to make a choice, or, exercise free will. If there is no choice, there can be no free will.

 Don't like the way that sounds? Don't like the fact that anyone could commit an act of evil towards you or someone you love, if they felt inclined to do so? Well let me ask you this? Would you be willing to give up your right to free will choice for security? Would you rather have been created like the Angels, programmed, and unable to choose your eternal fate? It's kind of a moot point because things were not done that way, but do you see where this is going? In order to have true love you must have free will. And along with that comes the possibility that some will not choose to exercise their free will in a way that benefits themselves, or mankind in a positive way.

 A risky move on Gods part, but a necessary move. Necessary in order for both him and us to experience a true free will love based relationship.

 Bet you've never heard this stuff in church before! 😜. And you won't. Why? Because this is considered radical stuff! And radicals are typically shunned. Sometimes that's a good thing. We have some religious radicals right now in our time running around killing people in the name of their religion. That's not what God is about folks. These acts are not of him nor condoned by him. Talk about the ultimate in misrepresentation! Well almost! What's worse is misleading people from truth in a way that keeps them from making that second choice. Which is the choice that gives them life; spiritual life. You can kill the body, which is temporal anyway, but when you prevent a person from hearing the truth that would have given them spiritual life, you're helping them to remain in a spiritual death, that one day, will be permanent. I don't want that on my conscience.

There are other types of misleaders. I'm going to call out one right now! Tele-evangelists. I told you I was going to be candid!   I'm talking about the ones who are preaching miracle based or prosperity based gospels. You've heard them;

"Give to us and God will bless you ten or a hundred fold!" Pray right and give to us and you'll get your miracle! God wants you to have a miracle! If you don't support us you're standing against God", and so on. "

It's sickening! To say the least. They prey on people who do not search for truth for themselves, but rely on so called spiritual leaders to tell them what truth is. It's unfortunate that so many people rely on these church leaders to seek and teach them truth, instead of searching for themselves. Because if they had of searched for themselves they would have read that Jesus said that a wicked and adulterous generation seeks a miraculous sign?! 😕 Now here is the son of God, he does miracles, many of them, but he says, do not seek them. Why? Because miracles are not faith based. And God set the stage for faith to be the way we approach him. Remember, he's God, he made the rules. When it takes a miracle or something outward for you to believe, faith has nothing to do with it.

 So then why did Jesus do miracles? He did them in his day because the third person of Gods tri-partate self had not yet been sent to mankind to instruct, and to reveal. Mankind up to that point and until Christ was resurrected, did not have the ability to have the life and nature of God in them, so it was not possible for mankind to understand or receive revelation. So a little something else was needed to prove a point, or, teach a lesson. That's not the case today. We have God the Holy Spirit available to each and every one of us today. He is the teacher, or revealer if you will, of spiritual truth. That is his job. We are not to worship him, or pray to him, his job is to be our spiritual tutor. Jesus said the Holy Spirit would only reveal one truth to us, truth regarding Christ and our position in Christ. Nothing more. Today misrepresentation falls into this category because some denominations are teaching that there is something more than just believing in Christ.

They teach you must also receive the Holy Spirit, and in doing so you will receive power. And that so called power manifests itself in things like, signs and wonders and the speaking in tongues of angels, according to these denominations. What they actually do, is push people away because they look silly! Heck, they look Crazy! They do not understand what Jesus and the other writers were saying so they sensationalize the gospel! They neglect to believe their own bibles regarding what the purpose of the Holy Spirit is for. And according to Jesus, the Holy Spirits sole job is to reveal Christ in us, and us in him. He goes on to say that the Holy Spirit will not speak of himself. He will not bring glory to himself. This is contrary to what these denominations would have you believe.

 Another reason for misrepresentation is the misunderstanding of how God deals and interacts with mankind. And the fact that he has dealt with us differently, at different times in history in order for us to learn certain things. These time periods are called dispensations. A simple explanation of what a dispensation is, is a period of time where God dealt with mankind, differently than in other periods, for very specific reasons. For example, there is a dispensation of law, and there is a dispensation of grace. And in each one God dealt differently with us, in order to teach us a specific truth in that time period that we can understand today. There are seven dispensational time periods as I see it.

1. <u>The dispensation of innocence</u>. This is the time period from the creation of man, to the fall of man. What we learn from this time period is that even though

mankind, Adam and Eve were created perfect, they could not remain that way on their own and just like Lucifer, fell prey to their week souls because they didn't have Gods life in their spirit keeping their souls from sin.

2. The dispensation self-rule. This is the time period from the fall of mankind, to the giving of the law to Moses on Mt Sinai. What we learn from this time period is that left unto ourselves, to govern ourselves, without Gods nature in us we fail miserably and our corruption just gets worse and worse.

3. The dispensation of law. This is the time period from the giving of the law to Moses, to the resurrection of Christ. What we learn from this time period is that even when we are given laws with which to live by, apart from Gods nature in us we cannot follow those laws. How many times have you heard or even said yourself, "God just tell me what to do and I'll do it!" God told the Israelites what to do, gave them laws, precise instructions on how to live sinless, but they couldn't do it and neither can we without Christ in us. Even with Christ in us, we struggle because our souls are influenced by the world around us and fights with our spirit for control.

4. The dispensation of grace. This time period started with the resurrection of Christ as is still in effect today. What we are hopefully learning in this time period, is that even when we utterly fail within ourselves, God's

grace is such that he still loves us and provides in Christ, our redemption, life in him. Since God paid for all sin, for all of mankind, through his son, Jesus Christ, any sin past, present or future is cancelled out by his death on the cross.

 No one knows how long this time period will be. It could end tomorrow, it could continue for another thousand years. We were not given any clues. I think this is purposeful doing on Gods part for a couple of reasons. First, to raise a BIG family! Anyone who hears this and wishes to join the family, can do so. Second, we humans, at least most of us are procrastinators; it helps to keep us from the mindset of waiting till the last minute before believing. This is so we won't miss out on learning opportunities while we still live on this earth.

 5. <u>The tribulation period</u>. This period will be the time from when God pulls believers from the earth, allows Satan to reign on earth, and will last one thousand years. This will be a tough time. But from what I understand about what is written regarding this time, if anyone during this time will believe, God will extend life to them. Still going to be a tough time for them though. The only way to avoid the tribulation period is to have believed during the dispensation of grace, which is now!

 6. <u>The reign of Christ on earth</u>. This time period will start at the end of the tribulation with the final defeat

of Satan, and will last one thousand years. It is said Christ will rule with an iron scepter during this time. I do not understand much more than this regarding this time period other than this too will be a difficult time for man. An interesting note here. Many today are saying the end of the world is near. I know based on these future dispensations that there is at least two thousand years before the end of the world. However, I would not want to be on this earth during any part of the 5th and 6th dispensations. Gonna be a bitch, that's fer shore! 😁

7. The final dispensation is labeled by the scriptures and is called, the "Dispensation of the fullness of times." This will be the time period that starts with the end of Christ's reign on earth, and will last for all eternity. I'm sure we will be learning who we are and living what we learn, for all eternity.

 The bottom line lesson we can glean from all of these time periods is that in and of ourselves, without Gods life and nature in us to be our compass and anchor, we cannot be who God intended us to be, nor can we experience the type of relationship he has for us if we wish to receive it.

 Now, back to miracles and what Jesus said about them, If you have kids it should be easier for you to understand a little of what he was saying. When you instruct your children regarding certain things, let's say safety for example, you want them to believe you for their own safety, right? What if they ignored your safety procedures and let themselves in harm's way? There are some things you just want them to trust you on. There will come a day when they will be able to understand your concerns and instructions. But until that day, for their sake, you hope that they will listen and heed your words for their own safety even if they don't understand the why of it.

Jesus knew that outward signs like miracles, would deter us from learning about him through faith and revelation. Yes we are spiritual beings, but we are also carnal fleshly beings. And we usually place more stock in carnal things than we do spiritual things because we can see and touch them. Jesus knew this, so he told us not to trust them nor seek them. One passage of the bible speaks about outer carnal acts of spirituality that were being used by folks in that day, here's what it says;

 "*though we speak in tongues of angles, yet have not love, we are but a clanging symbo*l."

 There are other sayings just like this but I want to focus on just this one for a second. What the writer is telling us is that even if we could speak in an angelic language, if it's not done in love, we're just making noise. It doesn't profit anything. It has been my experience that the practice of speaking in tongues today is nothing more than a show off of how spiritual the individual thinks they are; because it truly profits folks nothing. Many of them argue that they speak in tongues for their own edification and in private. They say it makes them feel spiritual. And even though the scriptures allow this practice, they also say that spirituality cannot be felt emotionally, heard or touched. So to me what's the point!

Historically it was used as a means of reaching other people that didn't speak the language the evangelist spoke. And it's also debated as to how that actually worked, whether the speaker actually spoke the different languages, or the hearer heard what the speaker was saying in their own language making it a hearing miracle and not a speaking miracle. Nevertheless, there was a specific reason for the spirit to use it and that was to reveal the gospel to ears that didn't understand the speaker's native language. Many today misread that verse and take it to mean that we should strive to speak in tongues! Blows my mind! I don't know how they can even begin to come up with that translation. The writer tells us that love is a better way because it does not build up the ego of the individual like the exercising of these activities can do.

Those very words of Jesus are in the very bibles that prosperity and miracle preachers read, and yet they ignore the instruction of not seeking miracles signs and wonders! How stupid is that?! ☹ That's a hard one for me to get over. It's like reading a map that is telling you to go right, and you decide it's telling you to go left! Why do they do this? It's simple really, they either do not believe Christ, and their gospel is intended for their prosperity, not yours! Or they do not understand the instruction and are teaching in ignorance. I will probably get slammed by the religious community for this book, but I don't care, somebody needs to call it like it is. Somebody needs to point the way to a relationship with God, apart from all of the wacky crap going on and being preached in many of our pulpits these days. I've had this book in mind for 20 years, and now it's time.

Contrary to popular belief, God really wants us to know him, personally. You can't know him personally if you're wrapped up in just what he can do. And if you are focused on his representatives, your perception of him will be very diluted and often greatly misunderstood.

Saying that leads me to another point, individuals who turn away from God because his people misrepresented him, are fools! 😕 I don't know any other way to say it. Harsh I know. I can't help it though! If you are dissatisfied with what a person either tells you, or their actions are immoral or wrong and they claim to represent God, why would you throw the baby out with the bath water?! Why not instead go directly to God, and seek him for yourself? To hell with these other people who claim to represent him, yet are misrepresenting him! That should not turn you away from him. I can see that it should rightfully turn you away from the folks doing these things, or from the churches where these things happen, but why God? Do people actually think God is telling these folks to say or do these incorrect and immoral things? Of course not. There is another answer.

Sometimes, not all the time but sometimes, people are looking for a way out of the religious atmosphere they are in. They don't like it, they're not comfortable with it, and they are looking for a way out. I actually fit that description! To a certain degree.

I have never liked organized religion. There, I said it! I told you I would be candid and honest didn't I? From the time I was a kid I never felt comfortable sitting in churches, singing hymns, doing the things you do when you go to church. I was bored with it most of the time and thought to myself, "is this really what God wants from us?" I hated that about myself! Felt guilty sometimes. But I could never shake it. It all seemed so redundant to me. Almost icky! Uncomfortable! You religious folks are probably hollering now,

"See, I told you he was a heretic!" He doesn't like church, must be the devil in him!

Funny thing though, I always wanted to know God. It never dawned on me to not believe there was a God and since there was a God, I wanted to know him! The adventure of doing that excited me! I wanted his companionship. Religion has misrepresented God to me many times. And I didn't like it, and I knew somehow something was wrong. But never, did it make me think there was either no God, or that I wanted nothing to do with him. I had a radar in me that was searching for truth. And eventually I understood why I felt that way. I did something about it. Started going straight to the source. I began to seek God on my own without input from other sources. I wanted to know him directly and not from someone else's perspective.

It is for this reason that I say that folks who turn away from God using the excuse of misrepresentation by his claimed followers, either really didn't want to know him to begin with, maybe they were forced to go to church, or they simply didn't know how to carry on getting to know him apart from the church, and it was easier to just quit trying when they were disappointed by the people leading them. Or, some tragedy occurred in their life and they experienced a temporary need to understand why and thought religion might have the answer. Let's face it, searching for and understanding spiritual matters can be a daunting endeavor. To say the least. But the way I look at it is, if I am to live for eternity in some capacity, then I want to know what that is. And I want to know the one responsible for that life. You will not be mis-lead if you are truly searching for truth. I gotta say it, I hear this all the time when I bring up this subject;

"I've searched for truth all my life and I get nothing!"
So I ask them, have read the bible as well as other forms
of literature, you prayed and searched and gone to
meetings and studied for years, and you still get
nothing? The response is almost always, yeah, I've done
all that. When in reality they never opened a bible or
any religious book to speak of, and they never made a
conscious decision to search for truth no matter the
cost. Or, they flipped through the beginning of the
bible, couldn't get through all the begats, and said to
hell with it this is ridiculous. Most people who claim to
have searched have never made an actual decent effort
to find truth. But they still say they have. You ask me
how do I know this? I know because God will not let
you go unlearned and in the dark if you are truly looking
for him. I am confident in this.
 If you do the actual research, be sincere, open your
heart to the possibility that you don't know anything
really, but you want to know truth, you want to know
him, be patient, and you will know. He will reveal
himself to you. It may be a bit at a time, because this is
a life-long endeavor, but God will not forsake you in
this. I promise.

 There is no law that says you have to attend church
every Sunday and Wednesday. No law that says you
have to have to read your bible every day and pray
every day and act all pious and subdued. None of these
acts are necessary to become a child of God. Only belief
in Christ gets you in the family. Our life in Christ makes

us who we are. But God does not take away or change our individual personality or expression. We are all different in this respect. And even though these acts are not necessary to become a child of God, just like in the physical world, where searching and learning has its rewards, so it does in spiritual matters. My child is my child no matter what he/she does. But if my child refuses to get to know me, they never will know me. And I will have no influence in their outward physical life. It's the same with God.

 Also, just like believing, it's your choice to search or not to search. Free will does not end when you believe. We are faced daily with decisions and life scenarios that require us to exercise our free will. And we don't always choose the right path. But we're learning, growing, and hopefully getting to know the author of life, love, happiness and family. Do not let the idiots in this world who misrepresent your Father in heaven turn you away from him. He loves you, wants to spend time with you. It's your choice, you can either not believe, and be on your own, separated from God, or you can believe and become a part of his family. And when you believe, if you do, you can either be an informed family member, or an ignorant one. Your peace, happiness and joy in this life, the physical one, will depend upon which way you choose.

So choose wisely grasshopper! ☺

CHAPTER 3

The word of God

I chose this topic to be one of the chapters in this book because of the importance of understanding what these four words, "The Word of God", mean!

You might be thinking,
"It means the bible right?" Simple, why devote a chapter to that? Well, if this is what you were thinking, that what I mean by the word of God being the bible or any other scriptures or writings out there, you would be wrong! And so were the religious people of Jesus' day, just like many are today.

Since the inception of the cannon of scripture in King James day by the theological scholars of that day, this has been extremely misunderstood. Today, I hear from the pulpits time and again, "read the word of God" and you will be enlightened and you will know truth. I've seen so many ministers, teachers, and lay people alike pick up their bibles and wave them around proclaiming it to be the word of God. They are wrong!

Now you probably really think I am a heretic! Don't ya? That's okay; hopefully as I explain my statement you will begin to understand why I say these things. And you will see that there is someone of much greater importance than myself who completely agrees, as you will see in a few minutes.

So let me repeat myself just for clarification. The Bible, as well as any other written letters, scriptures, or books pertaining to the things of God, whether they are true or not, cannot and should not be called the Word of God! Why not?

Simply put, this is instruction from none other than the Son of God himself!

At one point in Jesus' ministry he had a discussion with the most religious people of his day those being the Pharisees. The Pharisees were religious leaders in Jesus' day. They placed all importance on the written law handed down from Moses on Mt Sinai. Their law or, scriptures were the most important item to these religious folks. So much so that anything said against them or any questioning of them was considered to be blasphemous. These writings and laws became so much the life of these people that they were blinded to what these writings told them about God and his plans. You see they could see these words, touch them, they were real to them and in fact they became God to them!

In this conversation Jesus had with them he pointed out to them the error of what they were doing. He told them that they were wrong to believe that their eternal life came from these scriptures because they had come to the point of believing that complete adhering to the laws and instructions in them were the basis for their salvation. He told them that these scriptures, or writings, explained to them who were to come and be their salvation and because they placed so much importance on the written word, they missed the parts where these scriptures testified about him. The scriptures became more precious than gold to these people and they completely missed the point of them.

 This is also done today. Try going to a church today and say the bible is not the word of God! Just try it, I dare ya!   You will most likely be labeled a heretic and folks will treat you like you have some kind of infectious disease! Now before you label me a heretic, or think I have some kind of infectious disease, let me explain.

 Our bible today tells us what the word of God is. And it does not label itself as being such. What it does say, is that the Word of God was with God in the beginning, and the Word of God is a "Person". Go ahead; don't take my word for it, read it yourself. It says,

 "*In the beginning was the Word, the word was with God, the Word was God. He, was with God in the beginning.*" It goes on to say that "*Word became flesh, and made his dwelling among us*". So what the scriptures are telling us here is that Word of God is not only a person, but the Word of God **is** Christ.

I remember my religious days. My bible was my God during this time. So I know this happens a lot! We become so fixated on the scriptures, that it becomes easy to miss the person whom those scriptures are introducing us to. I was in that mode. My bible was all marked up, highlighting the scriptures that I felt were most important. I had become quite legalistic. I was searching more for what I was supposed to do and how I was supposed to act, rather than getting to know the one the scriptures spoke of.

We all make the mistake of reading things in the scriptures that are there solely to help us know the heart and mind of God. Instead, we attempt to apply what we read to our lives and we get caught up trying to understand how to live examples that were not meant for us to live by but rather, were intended to introduce us to God.

At that time I owned an old Toyota station wagon. It ran good but had some body issues. The rear hatch door leaked when it rained. One night we got home late and I forgot to remove my bible from the car and it was setting at the rear of the car right under the leaking door seals. Guess what happened! Your right, it rained hard that evening! The next day I went out to get my bible and what I found was a mess! It was soaked. I was bummed because it literally ruined it. I had spent at least four years marking up this bible just the way I wanted. Color coordinated highlights on many scriptures I felt were the most important to me.

I purchased a new bible within a couple days and took my old one and started the painstaking task of re-highlighting the same verses from the old bible to the new one. As I began this task a thought crossed my mind. Don't just re-highlight those same scriptures, re-read the bible and start from scratch. You see at this time as well, I was beginning to think something was missing in my life regarding spiritual matters. I had run across a little phrase here and there in the bible that had me confused. Phrases like, "In Christ". "In Him". "In the Beloved".

I didn't understand what that meant. What did it mean to be, "In Christ"? I remembered a preacher one time telling me about this but his explanation was very short and brief. He admitted he didn't understand it so he just left it alone. He never taught on the subject, said it was beyond our comprehension. So I listened to that voice in my head and changed my focus from the things I thought I should be doing, to what it meant to be, In Christ.

It was like I was reading a different book! And for several more years I searched and contemplated this notion, this idea of being in Christ and he in us that the bible itself was revealing. I began to understand Jesus' statements to the religious folks about them missing the whole point of the scriptures they so highly valued. Bit by bit I began to understand that our focus was not to be on the doing, but on a knowing.

Think about it like this, let's say you've never met your Dad, and he was a famous guy so you find a book written about him and his exploits etc. You read the book. But what you get out of it is thinking the book is designed to tell you how to live like your life and do the same things as your dad, not understanding that it's real purpose were for you to get to know him. To see how he handled certain situations. How he dealt with people in those different situations. How he operated and through those things that he said and did you got to know his heart and mind.

Do you see where I'm going with this? I began to understand that the point of the scriptures, as well as anything else written in regards to God, was always meant to be a tool used by us to get to know him. The Ten Commandments were not written for us to post on our walls and live by! No one can live by them. Not completely. They were written for two purposes. One, to prove to us that we could not live by them, and second, as a means of looking into the heart and mind of God. Knowing what a person likes and doesn't like helps in knowing that person doesn't it? Those commands are love commands. If you love your neighbor you won't kill them, or covet what they have etc. If you love God you won't seek other gods to worship, or deny that he exists. Through these commands God is saying, "This is who I am". These are some things I find important in order for there to be peace and harmony. He's also saying, "apart from you having my life and nature in you, you cannot live up to these standards. You need me, and I'm here for you!

I set my bible down after those last few yours of study, and learning of our position in Christ. I realized I wanted to understand these truths under real world experiences and with modern revelation. What I am saying is there is a time to put down the books we had in school and live life for real! Allowing the Spirit of God to take everyday circumstances and situations from this century, and teach us who we are. I haven't read from any bible in over 20 years. I have on my phone a bible software that maybe once or twice a year I will look up a verse I once read in order to explain to someone quoting that verse what it actually means.

There is nothing wrong with going through a period of time reading and studying old scriptures and writings in order to better know God. But to create a world, a lifestyle, out of these writings that does not fit today, or, does not lead you to a deeper relationship with God, and does not help you to understand who you are in Christ, is a misdirected life. Kind of like the career student who never leaves school. They never allow themselves to take the things they learned and to live life with their newfound knowledge.

The Word is a person. Learn what you can about him through what writings there are, and then take that knowledge into the adventure called life and allow the Spirit to reveal even more to you through the life you live today.

Printed in Great Britain
by Amazon